THE POETRY OF WAR

Edited by
Simon Fuller

Introduction

War poetry is often associated only with the experiences of those who fought, and sometimes died, in the First World War. Wilfrid Owen, Siegfried Sassoon, Isaac Rosenberg are just three of the hundreds of soldiers who chose to express their reactions to the carnage of trench warfare in verse. But war poetry is not exclusively male and the tradition did not end in 1918.

This anthology contains poems written from a wider perspective than just the soldier or the sailor, although there are plenty of those. Whole communities have been affected by recent wars. The whole world could be devastated by another world war. So there are poems here from the home front in the two world wars, Vietnam and the Falklands conflict. There are poems of protest and outrage about the nuclear threat and the war in Ireland.

The poems have been printed in a broadly chronological order to mirror the historical developments in each particular war. The original selection was made for a BBC School Radio series and the poems were set in the context of period songs and sound archives. Some of the poems, including those about the Falklands War, have not been published before.

These poems, with two or three exceptions, do not glorify war. They do recognise the sacrifices made in war and what war can do to people. They reflect the frequently bitter, occasionally witty, always tragic realities of war in the twentieth century.

The Choice of Poems

1914–1918

The first two poems reflect the patriotic fervour at the start of the war and the pressure on young men to enlist. As the recruitment progressed doubts began to emerge as to who was sacrificing what – and for whom.

At the front new recruits had difficulty adapting to the conditions of war, not least the lice, the rats, the mud, the gas and ultimately the incompetent leadership. Some were driven to desperate ends.

At home, many women took on paid employment for the first time and enjoyed a new freedom and a new prosperity. But when war finally ended there was much bitterness at the dreadful sacrifice.

The final poem is a reflection on the lasting images of the war.

1939–1945

The first section focuses on young people's experiences in the early stages of the war: a lot of uncertainty and mock heroics. The next section shows a mood of detachment and some cynicism amongst those preparing for war.

The war in the desert of North Africa yielded a lot of poetry that captured the spirit of that particular campaign. At sea also, one senses the grimness of a life and death struggle and a vulnerability in the face of increasingly powerful weaponry. Women were active in the war effort, nursing being but one of their many roles.

The war's victims, civilian and military, are considered in the final section.

1945–1989

The dropping of the atom bombs on Hiroshima and Nagasaki marked the dawning of the nuclear age and the arms race between the superpowers began. Although many warned of dire consequences, more and more nuclear weapons were stockpiled – enough to destroy the world many times over.

The likely effects of a nuclear war can be deduced from reading a number of these poems. Some people believe that nuclear weapons are necessary for maintaining world peace. Others have decided that trying to get rid of the weapons altogether is a more sensible and more hopeful strategy.

War in Our Time

VIETNAM: the horrors of the war, continuously reported in newspapers, on radio and TV, provoked world-wide protests, not least in the USA itself. The Americans were forced to pull out, but not without great cost to the Vietnamese and themselves. THE FALKLANDS: the first three poems offer the servicemen's view of the fighting; the next two the effect of the war on those in Britain. The final three poems suggest a mix of reactions to the war's outcomes. IRELAND: armed conflict, civilian casualties, sectarian murders – a killing cycle to the twenty years of fighting in Northern Ireland.

Contents

Introduction		2
The Choice of Poems		3
1914–1918 The First World War		

■ THE OUTBREAK OF WAR

Peace	Rupert Brooke	10
England To Her Sons	W. N. Hodgson	11

■ PREPARING FOR WAR

On Receiving News of the War*		
	Isaac Rosenberg	12
Recruiting*	E. A. Mackintosh	13
The Send-Off*	Wilfrid Owen	14

■ THE WAR FRONT

Breakfast*	Wilfrid Gibson	15
The Letter*	Wilfrid Owen	16
Louse Hunting	Isaac Rosenberg	18
The General*	Siegfried Sassoon	19
Dulce et Decorum Est*	Wilfrid Owen	20
Suicide in the Trenches*	Siegfried Sassoon	21
The Deserter	Winifred Letts	22

■ THE HOME FRONT

War Girls	Jessie Pope	23
Munition Wages*	Madeline Ida Bedford	24
Many Sisters To Many Brothers*		
	Rose Macaulay	25

■ THE AFTERMATH

Does It Matter?*	Siegfried Sassoon	26
OBE*	A. A. Milne	27
The Great War*	Vernon Scannell	28

1939–1945 The Second World War

■ THE BLACKOUT, THE BLITZ
AND EVACUATION

The Second World War*	Elizabeth Jennings	32
Autobiography	Adrian Henri	33
Children in Wartime*	Isobel Thrilling	34
Evacuee*	Isobel Thrilling	36

■ TRAINING

Bayonet Training	Vernon Scannell	38
Naming of Parts*	Henry Reed	39

■ WARFARE

LRDG*	J. G. Meddemmen	40
Lament of a Desert Rat	N. J. Trapnell	42
Elegy for an 88 Gunner*	Keith Douglas	44
So Long*	Hamish Henderson	46
Convoy Episode	John Wedge	47
Air Raid*	Charles Robinson	48

■ AT HOME

Air-Raid Casualties	Patricia Ledward	49
Lament*	Francis Mayo	50

■ VICTIMS OF WAR

Pigtail*	Tadeusz Różewicz	51
The Rain*	Zbigniew Herbert	52
Casualty – Mental Ward	Vernon Scannell	54
Post-War*	Libby Houston	55

1945–1989 Hiroshima and the Nuclear Age

■ HIROSHIMA AND NAGASAKI
August 6, 1945*   Alison Fell   59
August 10, 1945 – The Day After*
                                Edward Lowbury   60
No More Hiroshimas   James Kirkup   62

■ THE NUCLEAR THREAT
The Unexploded Bomb   C. Day Lewis   65
Military Two-Step   Cecil Rajendra   67
Icarus Allsorts*   Roger McGough   68
Inscribing the Circles*   Frank Flynn   70
Small Ad*   Rosemary Southey   71
Your Attention Please*   Peter Porter   72

■ PROTEST AND SURVIVAL
Refuse Cruise   Phil Vallack   74
In Favour of the Bomb   R. J. Latham   75
I Sing of Change*   Niyi Osundare   77
The Horses*   Edwin Muir   78

War in Our Time: Vietnam, Falklands, Ireland

■ THE VIETNAM WAR

Green Beret*	Ho Thien	82
What Were They Like?*	Denise Levertov	84
All Quiet*	David Ignatow	85
To Whom It May Concern	Adrian Mitchell	86
Casualty	Steve Mason	88

■ THE FALKLANDS WAR

Dawn Attack*	R. J. Latham	93
No Heroes*	David Morgan	95
My Family*	Paul D. Wapshott	96
Gotcha Drama	Katherine Gallagher	98
Tea-time in Portsmouth*	Margaret Hothi	99
Falkland Memorial Service Parade, Aldershot*	Jean Hathaway	100
We Shall Remember Them*	Sheila Parry	101
Tumbledown	Margaret J. Tiddy	102

■ IRELAND

Casualty*	Seamus Heaney	106
Site of Ambush	Eiléan Ni Chuilleanáin	108
The Toome Road	Seamus Heaney	110
The Identification*	Roger McGough	112
Wounds*	Michael Longley	114

Studying Poetry – Strategies and Assignments	117
Index of Authors	127

Poems marked with * are included on the cassette.

DON'T
IMAGINE
YOU
ARE NOT
WANTED

EVERY MAN
between 19 and 38
years of age
is WANTED!
Ex-Soldiers up
to 45 years of age

"YOUR COUNTRY NEEDS
YOU"

MEN CAN
ENLIST
IN THE
NEW
ARMY
FOR THE
DURATION
OF THE
WAR

RATE OF PAY: Lowest Scale 7s. per week with Food, Clothing &c., in addition

1. Separation Allowance for Wives and Children of Married Men when separated from their Families (Exclusive of the allotment received from the Soldier's pay of a maximum of 3d. a day in the case of a private)

For a Wife without Children · · 12s. 6d. per week
For Wife with One Child · · 15s. 6d. per week
For Wife with Two Children · · 17s. 6d. per week
For Wife with Three Children · · 20s. 0d. per week
For Wife with Four Children · · 22s. 0d. per week

and so on, with an addition of 2s. for each additional child.
Motherless children 5s. a week each, exclusive of allotment from Soldier's pay

2. Separation Allowance for Dependants of Unmarried Men.

Provided the Soldier does his share, the Government
will assist liberally in keeping up, within the limits
of Separation Allowance for Families, any regular
contribution made before enlistment by unmarried
Soldiers or Widowers to other dependants such as
mothers, fathers, sisters, etc.

YOUR COUNTRY IS STILL CALLING.
FIGHTING MEN!   FALL IN!!

Full Particulars can be obtained at any Recruiting Office or Post Office.

THE FIRST WORLD WAR

Britain declared war on Germany on 4 August 1914. Many thought the war would be over by Christmas and it was: Christmas, 1918. Troops from Britain, France, Italy, Russia and later the USA fought troops from Germany, Austro-Hungary and Turkey. There was fighting on land and sea, but the war is especially remembered for the trench warfare in western Europe. Ten million soldiers were killed and twenty-one million were wounded in the war. On the first day of the Battle of the Somme, 1 July 1916, 19,000 British troops were killed and 57,000 were wounded.

Women played a major role, taking on certain jobs in, for example, factories and transport.

Of the poets represented here, W. N. Hodgson, E. A. Mackintosh, Isaac Rosenberg and Wilfrid Owen were killed in the war. Rupert Brooke died from blood poisoning. Watching the victory celebrations in 1918, Siegfried Sassoon wrote: 'It is a loathsome ending to the loathsome tragedy of the last four years.'

Now, God be thanked Who has matched us with His hour,
    And caught our youth, and wakened us from sleeping,
With hand made sure, clear eye, and sharpened power,
    To turn, as swimmers into cleanness leaping,
Glad from a world grown old and cold and weary,
    Leave the sick hearts that honour could not move,
And half-men, and their dirty songs and dreary,
    And all the little emptiness of love!

Oh! we, who have known shame, we have found release there,
    Where there's no ill, no grief, but sleep has mending,
        Naught broken save this body, lost but breath;
Nothing to shake the laughing heart's long peace there
    But only agony, and that has ending;
        And the worst friend and enemy is but Death.

Rupert Brooke

Sons of mine, I hear you thrilling
To the trumpet call of war;
Gird ye then, I give you freely
As I gave your sires before,
All the noblest of the children I in love and anguish bore.

Free in service, wise in justice,
Fearing but dishonour's breath;
Steeled to suffer uncomplaining
Loss and failure, pain and death;
Strong in faith that sees the issue and in hope that triumpheth.

Go, and may the God of battles
You in His good guidance keep:
And if He in wisdom giveth
Unto His beloved sleep,
I accept it nothing asking, save a little space to weep.

W. N. Hodgson

On Receiving News of the War

Snow is a strange white word.
No ice or frost
Has asked of bud or bird
For Winter's cost.

Yet ice and frost and snow
From earth to sky
This Summer land doth know.
No man knows why.

In all men's hearts it is.
Some spirit old
Hath turned with maligned kiss
Our lives to mould.

Red fangs have torn His face.
God's blood is shed.
He mourns from His lone place
His children dead.

O! ancient crimson curse!
Corrode, consume.
Give back this universe
Its pristine bloom.

Isaac Rosenberg

'Lads, you're wanted, go and help',
On the railway carriage wall
Stuck the poster, and I thought
Of hands that penned the call.

Fat civilians wishing they
'Could go and fight the Hun.'
Can't you see them thanking God
That they're over forty-one?

Girls with feathers, vulgar songs –
Washy verse on England's need –
God – and don't we damned well know
How the message ought to read.

'Lads, you're wanted! over there',
Shiver in the morning dew,
More devils like yourselves
Waiting to be killed by you.

Go and help to swell the names
In the casualty lists.
Help to make a column's stuff
For the blasted journalists.

Help to keep them nice and safe
From the wicked German foe.
Don't let him come over here!
'Lads, you're wanted – out you go' . . .

Take your risk of life and death
Underneath the open sky.
Live clean or go out quick –
Lads, you're wanted. Come and die.

E. A. Mackintosh

Down the close darkening lanes they sang their way
To the siding-shed,
And lined the train with faces grimly gay.

Their breasts were stuck all white with wreath and spray
As men's are, dead.

Dull porters watched them, and a casual tramp
Stood staring hard,
Sorry to miss them from the upland camp.

Then, unmoved, signals nodded, and a lamp
Winked to the guard.

So secretly, like wrongs hushed-up, they went.
They were not ours:
We never heard to which front these were sent;

Nor there if they yet mock what women meant
Who gave them flowers.

Shall they return to beating of great bells
In wild train-loads?
A few, a few, too few for drums and yells,

May creep back, silent, to village wells,
Up half-known roads.

Wilfrid Owen

We ate our breakfast lying on our backs
Because the shells were screeching overhead.
I bet a rasher to a loaf of bread
That Hull United would beat Halifax
When Jimmy Stainthorpe played full-back instead
Of Billy Bradford. Ginger raised his head
And cursed, and took the bet, and dropt back dead.
We ate our breakfast lying on our backs
Because the shells were screeching overhead.

Wilfrid Gibson

With BEF* June 10. Dear Wife,
(O blast this pencil. 'Ere, Bill, lend's a knife.)
I'm in the pink at present, dear.
I think the war will end this year.
We don't see much of them square-'eaded 'Uns.
We're out of harm's way, not bad fed.
I'm longing for a taste of your old buns.
(Say, Jimmie, spare's a bite of bread.)
There don't seem much to say just now.
(Yer what? Then don't, yer ruddy cow!
And give us back me cigarette!)
I'll soon be 'ome. You mustn't fret.
My feet's improvin', as I told you of.
We're out in rest now. Never fear.
(VRACH! By crumbs, but that was near.)
Mother might spare you half a sov.
Kiss Nell and Bert. When me and you –
(Eh? What the 'ell! Stand to? Stand to!
Jim, give's a hand with pack on, lad.
Guh! Christ! I'm hit. Take 'old. Aye, bad.
No, damn your iodine. Jim? 'Ere!
Write my old girl, Jim, there's a dear.)

Wilfrid Owen

* British Expeditionary Force.

'It was just hell on earth. The guns never stopped. Shells never stopped, not hardly for a minute. There wasn't a flat bit of earth anywhere. Craters everywhere. Craters cutting the lips of other craters.'

BBC Archive

Nudes – stark and glistening,
Yelling in lurid glee. Grinning faces
And raging limbs
Whirl over the floor on fire.
For a shirt verminously busy
Yon soldier tore from his throat, with oaths
Godhead might shrink at, but not the lice.
And soon the shirt was aflare
Over the candle he'd lit while we lay.

Then we all sprang up and stript
To hunt the verminous brood.
Soon like a demons' pantomime
The place was raging.
See the silhouettes agape,
See the gibbering shadows
Mixed with the battled arms on the wall.
See gargantuan hooked fingers
Pluck in supreme flesh
To smutch supreme littleness.
See the merry limbs in hot Highland fling
Because some wizard vermin
Charmed from the quiet this revel
When our ears were half lulled
By the dark music
Blown from Sleep's trumpet.

Isaac Rosenberg

The General

'Good-morning; good-morning!' the General said
When we met him last week on our way to the Line.
Now the soldiers he smiled at are most of 'em dead,
And we're cursing his staff for incompetent swine.
'He's a cheery old card,' grunted Harry to Jack
As they slogged up to Arras with rifle and pack.

But he did for them both by his plan of attack.

Siegfried Sassoon

'That whole wood was lined with machine guns
from one end to the other. The company went
over 230 strong and only 11 privates survived.
This was ridiculous. It had never been
planned at all.'

BBC Archive

Dulce et Decorum Est

Bent double, like old beggars under sacks,
Knock-kneed, coughing like hags, we cursed through sludge,
Till on the haunting flares we turned our backs
And towards our distant rest began to trudge.
Men marched asleep. Many had lost their boots
But limped on, blood-shod. All went lame; all blind;
Drunk with fatigue; deaf even to the hoots
Of gas shells dropping softly behind.

Gas! GAS! Quick, boys! – An ecstasy of fumbling,
Fitting the clumsy helmets just in time;
But someone still was yelling out and stumbling,
And flound'ring like a man in fire or lime . . .
Dim, through the misty panes and thick green light,
As under a green sea, I saw him drowning.

In all my dreams, before my helpless sight,
He plunges at me, guttering, choking, drowning.

If in some smothering dreams you too could pace
Behind the wagon that we flung him in,
And watch the white eyes writhing in his face,
His hanging face, like a devil's sick of sin;
If you could hear, at every jolt, the blood
Come gargling from the froth-corrupted lungs,
Obscene as cancer, bitter as the cud
Of vile, incurable sores on innocent tongues, –
My friend, you would not tell with such high zest
To children ardent for some desperate glory,
The old Lie: Dulce et decorum est
Pro patria mori.

Wilfrid Owen

Suicide in the Trenches

I knew a simple soldier boy
Who grinned at life in empty joy,
Slept soundly through the lonesome dark,
And whistled early with the lark.

In winter trenches, cowed and glum,
With crumps and lice and lack of rum,
He put a bullet through his brain.
No one spoke of him again.

You smug-faced crowds with kindling eye
Who cheer when soldier lads march by,
Sneak home and pray you'll never know
The hell where youth and laughter go.

Siegfried Sassoon

There was a man, – don't mind his name,
Whom Fear had dogged by night and day.
He could not face the German guns
And so he turned and ran away.
Just that – he turned and ran away,
But who can judge him, you or I?
God makes a man of flesh and blood
Who yearns to live and not to die.
And this man when he feared to die
Was scared as any frightened child,
His knees were shaking under him,
His breath came fast, his eyes were wild.
I've seen a hare with eyes as wild,
With throbbing heart and sobbing breath.
But oh! it shames one's soul to see
A man in abject fear of death.
But fear had gripped him, so had death;
His number had gone up that day,
They might not heed his frightened eyes,
They shot him when the dawn was grey.
Blindfolded, when the dawn was grey,
He stood there in a place apart,
The shots rang out and down he fell,
An English bullet in his heart.
An English bullet in his heart!
But here's the irony of life, –
His mother thinks he fought and fell
A hero, foremost in the strife.
So she goes proudly; to the strife
Her best, her hero son she gave.
O well for her she does not know
He lies in a deserter's grave.

Winifred Letts

There's the girl who clips your ticket for the train,
And the girl who speeds the lift from floor to floor,
There's the girl who does a milk-round in the rain,
And the girl who calls for orders at your door.
Strong, sensible, and fit,
They're out to show their grit,
And tackle jobs with energy and knack.
No longer caged and penned up,
They're going to keep their end up
Till the khaki soldier boys come marching back.

There's the motor girl who drives a heavy van,
There's the butcher girl who brings your joint of meat,
There's the girl who cries 'All fares, please!' like a man,
And the girl who whistles taxis up the street.
Beneath each uniform
Beats a heart that's soft and warm,
Though of canny mother-wit they show no lack;
But a solemn statement this is,
They've no time for love and kisses
Till the khaki soldier boys come marching back.

Jessie Pope

Earning high wages? Yus,
　　Five quid a week.
A woman, too, mind you,
　　I calls it dim sweet.

Ye'are asking some questions –
　　But bless yer, here goes:
I spends the whole racket
　　On good times and clothes.

Me saving? Elijah!
　　Yer do think I'm mad.
I'm acting the lady,
　　But – I ain't living bad.

I'm having life's good times.
　　See 'ere, it's like this:
The 'oof come o' danger,
　　A touch-and-go bizz.

We're all here today, mate,
　　Tomorrow – perhaps dead,
If Fate tumbles on us
　　And blows up our shed.

Afraid! Are yer kidding?
　　With money to spend!
Years back I wore tatters,
　　Now – silk stockings, mi friend!

I've bracelets and jewellery,
　　Rings envied by friends;
A sergeant to swank with,
　　And something to lend.

I drive out in taxis,
　　Do theatres in style.
And this is mi verdict –
　　It is jolly worth while.

Worth while, for tomorrow
　　If I'm blown to the sky,
I'll have repaid mi wages
　　In death – and pass by.

Madeline Ida Bedford

Many Sisters To Many Brothers

When we fought campaigns (in the long Christmas rains)
  With soldiers spread in troops on the floor,
I shot as straight as you, my losses were as few,
  My victories as many, or more.
And when in naval battle, amid cannon's rattle,
  Fleet met fleet in the bath,
My cruisers were as trim, my battleships as grim,
  My submarines cut as swift a path.
Or, when it rained too long, and the strength of the strong
  Surged up and broke a way with blows,
I was as fit and keen, my fists hit as clean,
  Your black eye matched my bleeding nose.
Was there a scrap or ploy in which you, the boy,
  Could better me? You could not climb higher,
Ride straighter, run as quick (and to smoke made you sick)
. . . But I sit here and you're under fire.

Oh, it's you that have the luck, out there in blood and muck:
  You were born beneath a kindly star;
All we dreamt, I and you, you can really go and do,
  And I can't, the way things are.
In a trench you are sitting, while I am knitting
  A hopeless sock that never gets done.
Well, here's luck, my dear; – and you've got it, no fear;
  But for me . . . a war is poor fun.

Rose Macaulay

Does it matter? – losing your legs? . . .
For people will always be kind,
And you need not show that you mind
When the others come in after hunting
To gobble their muffins and eggs.

Does it matter? – losing your sight? . . .
There's such splendid work for the blind;
And people will always be kind,
As you sit on the terrace remembering
And turning your face to the light.

Do they matter? – those dreams from the pit? . . .
You can drink and forget and be glad,
And people won't say that you're mad;
For they'll know that you've fought for your country
And no one will worry a bit.

Siegfried Sassoon

I know a Captain of Industry,
Who made big bombs for the RFC,
And collared a lot of £ s. d. –
And he – thank God! – has the OBE.

I know a Lady of Pedigree,
Who asked some soldiers out to tea,
And said 'Dear me!' and 'Yes, I see' –
And she – thank God! – has the OBE.

I know a fellow of twenty-three,
Who got a job with a fat MP –
(Not caring much for the Infantry.)
And he – thank God! – has the OBE.

I had a friend; a friend, and he
Just held the line for you and me,
And kept the Germans from the sea,
And died – without the OBE.
               Thank God!
He died without the OBE.

A. A. Milne

Whenever war is spoken of
I find
The war that was called Great invades the mind:
The grey militia marches over land
A darker mood of grey
Where fractured tree-trunks stand
And shells, exploding, open sudden fans
Of smoke and earth.
Blind murders scythe
The deathscape where the iron brambles writhe;
The sky at night
Is honoured with rosettes of fire,
Flares that define the corpses on the wire
As terror ticks on wrists at zero hour.
These things I see,
But they are only part
Of what it is that slyly probes the heart:
Less vivid images and words excite
The sensuous memory
And, even as I write
Fear and a kind of love collaborate
To call each simple conscript up
For quick inspection:
Trenches' parapets
Paunchy with sandbags; bandoliers, tin-hats,
Candles in dug-outs,
Duckboards, mud and rats.
Then, like patrols, tunes creep into the mind:
A Long Long Trail, The Rose of No-Man's Land,
Home Fires and *Tipperary*;
And through the misty keening of a band
Of Scottish pipes the proper names are heard
Like fateful commentary of distant guns;
Passchendaele, Bapaume, and Loos, and Mons.

And now,
Whenever the November sky
Quivers with a bugle's hoarse, sweet cry,
The reason darkens; in its evening gleam
Crosses and flares, tormented wire, grey earth
Splattered with crimson flowers,
And I remember,
Not the war I fought in
But the one called Great
Which ended in a sepia November
Four years before my birth.

Vernon Scannell

THE SECOND WORLD WAR

The 1939–1945 war was genuinely a global war with fighting occurring across the world, on land, at sea and in the air. Tanks, aeroplanes and submarines were the machines of war. British troops were mostly involved in Europe, North Africa and the Far East. At home, cities were bombed, in what is called the Blitz and children were sent off to live in the country. The worst civilian casualties occurred in Europe, where an estimated ten million were systematically killed in the Nazi concentration camps.

The war in Europe ended in May 1945. In the Far East it did not end until August after atomic bombs had been dropped on the Japanese cities of Hiroshima and Nagasaki.

Forty-five million people lost their lives in the Second World War, including twenty million Russians, seven million Germans and 400,000 British. The majority of deaths were civilian, which tells us something of the kind of war it was.

Daily Express

WORLD'S LARGEST DAILY SALE

No. 12,258   Monday, September 4, 1939

"We fight against evil things—brute force, bad faith, injustice, oppression and persecution—and against them I am certain that the right will prevail."—The Premier to Britain yesterday

FLEET BEGINS
THE BLOCKADE

STOP PRESS
WAR NEWS
Central 6000

WINSTON BACK

He is First Lord; Eden is the new Dominions Secretary

By GUY EDEN
Daily Express Political Correspondent

SEPTEMBER
3
SUNDAY

● AT 11 O'CLOCK yesterday morning Britain declared that a state of war existed between this country and Germany.

All ships searched : convoys started

POLES BEAT GERMANS BACK INTO *GERMANY*

BᴿITAIN'S NAVY STARTED THE BLOCKADE OF GERMANY LAST NIGHT. TWO RADIOGRAMS OF ONE CODE WORD EACH PUT THE WHOLE FLEET ON A WAR FOOTING. THE FIRST PROCLAIMED A STATE OF TENSION : THE SECOND TOLD EACH COMMANDER : "BEGIN HOSTILITIES!"

The Fleet in northern waters and in the Atlantic are concerned

FOUR PRISONERS ESCAPE

CZECH LEADERS SAY "WE ARE WITH YOU"

The voice said 'We are at War'
And I was afraid, for I did not know what this meant.
My sister and I ran to our friends next door
As if they could help. History was lessons learnt
With ancient dates, but here

Was something utterly new,
The radio, called the wireless then, had said
That the country would have to be brave. There was much to do.
And I remember that night as I lay in bed
I thought of soldiers who

Had stood on our nursery floor
Holding guns, on guard and stiff. But war meant blood
Shed over battle-fields, Cavalry galloping. War
On that September Sunday made us feel frightened
Of what our world waited for.

Elizabeth Jennings

'I am speaking to you from the cabinet room of ten
Downing Street. This morning the British ambassador
in Berlin handed the German government a final note
stating that unless we heard from them by eleven
o'clock, that they were prepared at once to withdraw
their troops from Poland, a state of war would exist
between us. I have to tell you now that no such
undertaking has been received and that consequently
this country is at war with Germany.'

**BBC Archive: radio announcement, on the day
that war was declared, by Prime Minister
Neville Chamberlain**

Carrying my gas-mask to school every day
buying saving stamps
remembering my National Registration Number
(ZMGM/136/3 see I can still remember it)
avoiding Careless Talk Digging for Victory
looking for German spies everywhere
Oh yes, I did my bit for my country that long dark winter,
me and Winston and one or two others,
wearing my tin hat whenever possible
Singing 'Hang out the Washing on the Siegfried Line'
aircraft-recognition charts pinned to my bedroom wall
the smell of paint on toy soldiers
doing paintings of Spitfires and Hurricanes,
                          Lancasters and Halifaxes
along with a Heinkel or a Messerschmitt plunging
                          helplessly into the sea in the background

pink light in the sky from Liverpool burning fifty miles away
the thunder of daylight flying fortresses high overhead
                          shaking the elderberry tree
bright barrage-balloons flying over the docks
morning curve of the bay seen from the park on the hill
after coming out of the air-raid shelter
listening for the 'All Clear' siren
listening to Vera Lynn Dorothy Lamour Allan Jones and the
    Andrews Sisters
clutching my father's hand tripping over the unfamiliar kerb
I walk over every day
in the black-out.

Adrian Henri

Children in Wartime

Sirens ripped open
the warm silk of sleep;
we ricocheted to the shelter
moated by streets
that ran with darkness.
People said it was a storm,
but flak
had not the right sound
for rain;
thunder left such huge craters
of silence,
we knew this was no giant
playing bowls.
And later,
when I saw the jaw of glass,
where once had hung
my window spun with stars;
it seemed the sky
lay broken on my floor.

Isobel Thrilling

A case stood in the hall
outlining the weight
of fear,
her doll felt cold,
she knew then
it had always been dead.
She left it
on the pillow,
heir to the wall-paper
roses and woolly dog.

Shadows clung
to her clothes at the door;
light struck bone.
She walked unshaded
down streets,
climbed a train and watched
the receding
lamps of platform faces.

The lady was kind,
wove stories
with tinsel thread;
but the texture
of her voice was strange,
her mouth
seemed painted on wax;
the smile ran red.

Isobel Thrilling

From far away, a mile or so,
The wooden scaffolds could be seen
On which fat felons swung;
But closer view showed these to be
Sacks, corpulent with straw and tied
To beams from which they hung.

The sergeant halted his platoon.
'Right lads,' he barked, 'you see them sacks?
I want you to forget
That sacks is what they are and act
As if they was all Jerries – wait!
Don't move a muscle yet!

'I'm going to show you how to use
The bayonet as it should be done.
If any of you feel
Squeamish like, I'll tell you this:
There's one thing Jerry just can't face
And that thing is cold steel.

'So if we're going to win this war
You've got to understand you must
Be brutal, ruthless, tough.
I want to hear you scream for blood
As you rip out his guts and see
The stuff he had for duff.'

The young recruits stood there and watched
And listened as their tutor roared
And stabbed his lifeless foe;
Their faces were expressionless,
Impassive as the winter skies
Black with threats of snow.

Vernon Scannell

Naming of Parts

Today we have naming of parts. Yesterday,
We had daily cleaning. And to-morrow morning,
We shall have what to do after firing. But to-day,
To-day we have naming of parts. Japonica
Glistens like coral in all of the neighbouring gardens
   And today we have naming of parts.

This is the lower sling swivel. And this
Is the upper sling swivel, whose use you will see
When you are given your slings. And this is the piling swivel,
Which in your case you have not got. The branches
Hold in the gardens their silent, eloquent gestures,
   Which in our case we have not got.

This is the safety-catch, which is always released
With an easy flick of the thumb. And please do not let me
See anyone using his finger. You can do it quite easy
If you have any strength in your thumb. The blossoms
Are fragile and motionless, never letting anyone see
   Any of them using their finger.

And this you can see is the bolt. The purpose of this
Is to open the breech, as you can see. We can slide it
Rapidly backwards and forwards; we call this
Easing the spring. And rapidly backwards and forwards
The early bees are assaulting and fumbling the flowers:
   They call it easing the Spring.

They call it easing the Spring; it is perfectly easy
If you have any strength in your thumb: like the bolt,
And the breech, and the cocking-piece, and the point of balance,
Which in our case we have not got; and the almond-blossom
Silent in all of the gardens and the bees going backwards and
   forwards,
   For today we have naming of parts.

Henry Reed

He threw his cigarette in silence, then he said:

You can't predict in war;
It's a matter of luck, nothing less, nothing more.
Now here's an instance. Darnley copped it in the head
His third day up the blue although he'd seen the lot
In Dunkerque, Greece and Crete –
The sort that went in tidy and came out neat;
He copped it when the going wasn't even hot.
And there was little Pansy Flowers,
Machine-gunned through the guts; he bled
(And not a murmur from him) for hours
Before he jagged it in.

                              And you remember Bowers?
Bowers got fragmentation in the lungs and thigh;
We couldn't do a thing: the moon was high
And a hell of a bright
On that particular night.
Poor sod, he won't kip in a civvy bed.

It's queer . . . I've even laughed
When blokes have chucked it in and gone daft.
I remember one that scarpered bollock-nude
One midnight, out across the dunes, calling for Mum;
You'd have thought him blewed.
He wasn't seen again – not this side of Kingdom Come.

One job that I really funked
Was when Fat Riley bunked
From a Jerry leaguer on a getaway.
We found him blind, with both hands gone.
When we got him back inside the lines
He'd only say,
Over and over, 'the mines, the mines, the mines'.
It's the lucky ones get dead:
He's still alive. I wonder if his wife understands
How you can't even shoot yourself without your hands.

March 1942.

J. G. Meddemmen

*Long Range Desert Group.

Lament of a Desert Rat

I've learnt to wash in petrol tins, and shave myself in tea
Whilst balancing the fragments of a mirror on my knee
I've learnt to dodge the eighty-eights, and flying lumps of lead
And to keep a foot of sand between a Stuka and my head
I've learnt to keep my ration bag crammed full of buckshee food
And to take my Army ration, and to pinch what else I could
I've learnt to cook my bully-beef with candle-ends and string
In an empty petrol can, or any other thing
I've learnt to use my jack-knife for anything I please
A bread-knife, or a chopper, or a prong for toasting cheese
I've learnt to gather souvenirs, that home I hoped to send
And hump them round for months and months, and dump them
    in the end
But one day when this blooming war is just a memory
I'll laugh at all these troubles, when I'm drifting o'er the sea
But until that longed-for day arrives, I'll have to be content
With bully-beef and rice and prunes, and sleeping in a tent.

N. J. Trapnel

Elegy for an 88 Gunner*

Three weeks gone and the combatants gone,
returning over the nightmare ground
we found the place again and found
the soldier sprawling in the sun.

The frowning barrel of his gun
overshadows him. As we came on
that day, he hit my tank with one
like the entry of a demon.

And smiling in the gunpit spoil
is a picture of his girl
who has written: *Steffi, Vergissmeinicht.*
in a copybook Gothic script.

We see him almost with content,
abased and seeming to have paid,
mocked by his durable equipment
that's hard and good when he's decayed.

But she would weep to see today
how on his skin the swart flies move,
the dust upon the paper eye
and the burst stomach like a cave.

For here the lover and the killer are mingled
who had one body and one heart;
and Death, who had the soldier singled
has done the lover mortal hurt.

Home, Tripolitania, 1943.

Keith Douglas

*Published elsewhere under the title 'Vergissmeinicht'.

(Recrossing the Sollum Frontier from Libya into Egypt, 22nd May, 1943, in a lorry carrying captured enemy equipment.)

To the war in Africa that's over – goodnight.
    To thousands of assorted vehicles, in every stage of
      decomposition,
    littering the desert from here to Tunis – goodnight.
To thousands of guns and armoured fighting vehicles
    brewed up, blackened and charred
from Alamein to here, from here to Tunis – goodnight.
To thousands of crosses of every shape and pattern,
    alone or in little huddles, under which the unlucky bastards
      lie –
      goodnight

        Horse-shoe curve of the bay,
      clean razor-edge of the escarpment,
    tonight it's the sunset only that's blooding you.

Halfaya and Sollum: I think that at long last
    we can promise you a little quiet.

So long. I hope I won't be seeing you.

To the sodding desert – you know what you can do with
    yourself.

To the African deadland – God help you – and goodnight.

Hamish Henderson

No sound save swishing sea is heard
Above the throb of engines. Ships
To starboard silently pursue
Their course; a single seagull dips
Astern, and dusk and the grey gloom
Steal ever closer from the dim
Horizon . . . . Mute, be-duffeled men
Stand grouped around their guns, as grim
As gravestones, peering eastward for
That shape which spells a welcome chance
Of action . . . Heroes? No – beneath
Each muffled frame a heart a-dance
And stomach sickly strained
With apprehensive tension.
                                        Then . . .
'Aircraft in sight!' The air at once
Is full of sound, alive again,
The pom-poms pumping death, swift red
Tracked tracer tears the sky,
Staccato clatter marks the quick
Fed Bren; green beaded streams let fly
From other guns, ship shakes as shells
Are hurled from major armament –
Exhilarating cordite fumes
Escape as every charge is spent.
The Heinkel hesitates, then twists
And disappears beneath the swell . . .
A cheer. . .
                    'Cease fire'. . .
                                        A happy crew
Collects the case of every shell
Expended – souvenirs, as were
The boxing programmes years ago –
The thrill of victory the same
And joy of contest. Well they know
The penalty for aiming low.

John Wedge

'Aircraft! Stand still you bloody fool.'
Too late. He's seen the movement and glittering in the sun.
The Messerschmidt swoops down with flame-tipped guns.
Around your sprawling form the deadly bullets splatter,
And lying tense fearful of the hideous chatter,
You feel Death's haunting figure stalking near,
Sweat, cold about your body, tingling with fear.

And now the plane has turned to its patrol.
You rise and fingers trembling light a cigarette.
One man lies groaning, arm smashed by a cannon-shell.
You pad a splint and bandage the jagged hole;
Now for the morphine, tell him not to fret,
He's bloody lucky he got off so well.

Charles Robinson

from
Air-Raid Casualties:
Ashridge Hospital

On Sundays friends arrive with kindly words
To peer at those whom war has crushed;
They bring the roar of health into these hushed
And solemn wards –
The summer wind blows through the doors and cools
The sweating forehead; it revives
Memories of other lives
Spent lying in the fields, or by sea-pools;
And ears that can discern
Only the whistling of a bomb it soothes
With tales of water splashing into smooth
Deep rivers fringed with ferns.
Nurses with level eyes, and chaste
In long starched dresses, move
Amongst the maimed, giving love
To strengthen bodies gone to waste.
The convalescents have been wheeled outside,
The sunshine strikes their cheeks and idle fingers,
Bringing to each a sensuous languor
And sentimental sorrow for the dead.

One by one the wards empty, happiness goes,
The hospital routine, the usual work
Return for another week;
The patients turn upon themselves, a hundred foes
Imagined swell their suffering;
Fretfully hands pick at sheets
And voices meet
Discussing symptoms and the chance of living.
Only the soldier lies remote and resolutely sane,
Remembering how, a boy, he dreamt of folk
With footballs. Maturity dispelled the dream – he woke
To know that he would never walk again.

Patricia Ledward

We knelt on the rocks by the dark green pools
The sailor boy and I,
And we dabbled our hands in the weed-veined water
Under a primrose sky.
And we laughed together to hide the sorrow
Of words we left unsaid;
Then he went back to his dirty minesweeper
And I to a lonely bed.
O the anguish of tears unshed.

And never again on this earth shall we meet,
The sailor boy and I,
And never again shall I see his face
Framed in a primrose sky,
For the sea has taken his laughter and loving
And buried him dark and deep
And another lad sleeps on the dirty minesweeper
A sleep that I cannot sleep.
O that I could forget and weep.

Frances Mayo

When all the women in the transport
had their heads shaved
four workmen with brooms made of birch twigs
swept up
and gathered up the hair

Behind clean glass
the stiff hair lies
of those suffocated in gas chambers
there are pins and side combs
in this hair

The hair is not shot through with light
is not parted by the breeze
is not touched by any hand
or rain or lips

In huge chests
clouds of dry hair
of those suffocated
and a faded plait
a pigtail with a ribbon
pulled at school
by naughty boys.

The Museum, Auschwitz, 1948.

Tadeusz Różewicz

Trans. Adam Czerniawski

When my older brother
came back from war
he had on his forehead a little silver star
and under the star
an abyss

a splinter of shrapnel
hit him at Verdun
or perhaps at Grünwald
(he'd forgotten the details)

he used to talk much
in many languages
but he liked most of all
the language of history

he shouted
that this was the last crusade
that Carthage soon would fall
and then sobbing confessed
that Napoleon did not like him

we looked at him
getting paler and paler
abandoned by his senses
he turned slowly into a monument

they took my brother
and carried him out of town
he returns every fall
slim and very quiet
(he does not want to come in)
he knocks at the window for me

we walk together in the streets
and he recites to me
improbable tales
touching my face
with blind fingers of rain

Zbigniew Herbert

Trans. Czeslaw Milosz

Casualty – Mental Ward

Something has gone wrong inside my head.
The sappers have left mines and wire behind;
I hold long conversations with the dead.

I do not always know what has been said;
The rhythms, not the words, stay in my mind;
Something has gone wrong inside my head.

Not just the sky but grass and trees are red,
The flares and tracers – or I'm colour-blind;
I hold long conversations with the dead.

Their presence comforts and sustains like bread;
When they don't come it's hard to be resigned;
Something has gone wrong inside my head.

They know about the snipers that I dread
And how the world is booby-trapped and mined;
I hold long conversations with the dead;

As all eyes close, they gather round my bed
And whisper consolation. When I find
Something has gone wrong inside my head
I hold long conversations with the dead.

Vernon Scannell

In 1943
my father
dropped bombs on the continent

I remember
my mother
talking about bananas
in 1944

when it rained,
creeping alone to the windowsill,
I stared up the hill,
watching, watching,
watching without a blink
for the Mighty Bananas
to stride through the blitz

they came in paper bags
in neighbours' hands
when they came
and took their time
over the coming

and still I don't know
where my father
flying home
took a wrong turning

Libby Houston

ROSHIMA AND THE NUCLEAR AGE

In order to bring the war with Japan to a quick end the Americans announced that they would use the atomic bomb if Japan failed to surrender. Japan either did not understand or did not believe the threat. On 6 August 1945 the bomb called 'Little Boy' was dropped on Hiroshima from a US plane called Enola Gay. On 9 August the second bomb 'Fat Man' was dropped on Nagasaki. The Japanese surrendered on 14 August. The Second World War was over. The Nuclear Age had just begun.

- **Hiroshima** – Population: **350,000**
Deaths by 1 November: **130,000**
- **Nagasaki** – Population: **270,000**
Deaths by 1 November: **65,000**
- Three-quarters of these deaths occurred on the first day.
- Two-thirds of all buildings were destroyed.

(Figures from *Medical Effect of Nuclear War* – British Medical Association.)

DAILY EXPRESS

No: 14,094 Lighting-up: 9.39 pm to 6.33 am TUESDAY AUGUST 7 1945 Weather: Cool, showers One (Penny)

Smoke hides city 16 hours · after greatest secret weapon strikes

THE BOMB THAT HAS CHANGED THE WORLD

Japs told 'Now quit'   20,000 tons in golf ball

THE Allies disclosed last night that they have used against Japan the most fearful device of war yet produced—an atomic bomb.

It was dropped at 20 minutes past midnight, London time, yesterday on the Japanese port and army base of Hiroshima, 190 miles west of Kobe.

The city was blotted out by a cloud of dust and smoke. Sixteen hours later

reconnaissance pilots were still waiting for the cloud to lift to let them see what had happened.

The bomb was a last warning. Now leaflets will tell the Japanese what to expect unless their Government surrenders.

So great will be the devastation if they do not surrender that Allied land forces may be able to invade without opposition.

ONE atomic bomb has a destructive force equal to that of 20,000 tons of T.N.T., or five 1,000-plane raids. This terrific power is packed in a space of little more than golf ball size.

Experts estimate that the bomb can destroy anything on the surface in an area of at least two square miles—twice the size of the City of London.

When it was tested after being assembled in a farmhouse in the remote desert of New Mexico, a steel tower used for the experiment vaporised; two men standing nearly six miles away were blown down; blast effect was felt 300 miles away.

And, at Albuquerque, 120 miles away, a blind girl cried "What is that?" when the flash lighted the sky before the explosion could be heard.

In God's mercy we outran Germany

This statement was prepared by Mr. Churchill before he resigned, and was issued from Downing-street last night.

By WINSTON S. CHURCHILL

BY THE YEAR 1939 IT HAD BECOME WIDELY RECOGNISED AMONG SCIENTISTS OF MANY NATIONS THAT THE RELEASE OF ENERGY BY ATOMIC FISSION

The men who knew

BLAST FELT 300 MILES FROM BOMB TEST

Steel tower turned to vapour

From C. V. R. THOMPSON: New York, Monday

THERE is reason to believe that the vital part of the atomic bomb with its almost incredible power of devastation is not much bigger than a golf ball.

We have not seen it; all that is given officially . . . THANKS

'When a nuclear bomb falls it's not just the people who die. It's the community that dies. Suddenly, in an instant, there's nothing but a desert of rubble and a jungle of dazed and frightened people coming out of hiding. All is shattered in a moment. I saw it shattered at Hiroshima and Nagasaki.'

BBC Archive: Dr Jacob Bronowski

August 6, 1945

In the Enola Gay
five minutes before impact
he whistles a dry tune
Later he will say
that the whole blooming sky
went up like an apricot ice
Later he will laugh and tremble
at such a surrender
for the eye of his belly
saw Marilyn's skirt's
fly over her head for ever

On the river bank
bees drizzle over
hot white rhododendrons
Later she will walk
the dust, a scarlet girl
with her whole stripped skin
at her heel, stuck like an old
shoe sole or mermaid's tail

Later she will lie down
in the flecked black ash
where the people are become
as lizards or salamanders
and, blinded, she will complain:
Mother you are late, so late

Later in dreams he will look
down shrieking and see
ladybirds
ladybirds

Alison Fell

Who will be next to break this terrible silence,
While the doom of war still shivers over these
Unwilling either to die or to be defeated, –
In the agony of death still torn, contorted,
Torn between saving face and body, both
Mutilated almost beyond recognition?
The face fights on long after
The body's overwhelmed and hacked to pieces.
Every scar of it's their fault; yet I am dumb;
In the blind eyes of pity the good and the evil
Are equals when they're gasping in the sand,
Helpless. The reality so blinds
Our senses that it seems less than a dream,
Yet we shall live to say 'Twice in a lifetime
We saw such nakedness that shame
Itself could not look on, and of all the feelings,
Hate, anger, justice, vengeance, violence, –
Horror alone remained, its organ voice
Searching us with a sickening clarity.'
And now the word comes in of those two cities
With all their living burden
Blown to the wind by power
Unused except by God at the creation, –
Atomised in the flash of an eye.
Who else but God or the instrument of God
Has the power to pass such sentence?
Here the road forks, to survival or extinction,
And I hold my tongue through the awful silence,
For if God had nothing to do with it,
Extinction is the least price man can pay.

                                   Edward Lowbury

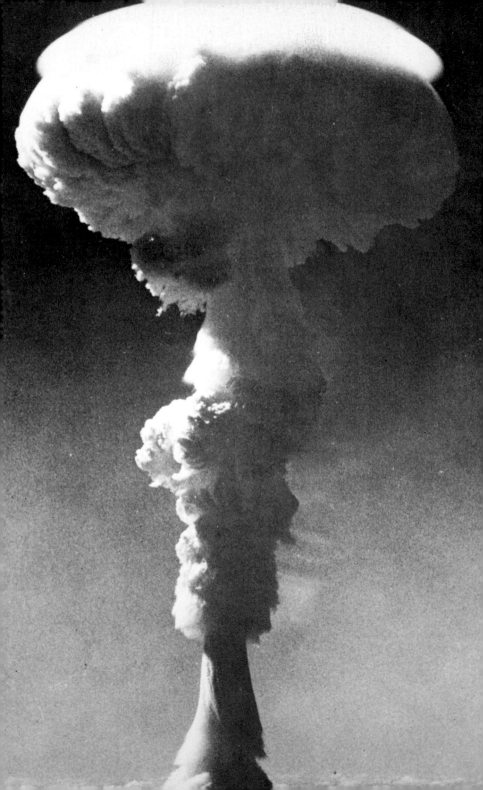

No More Hiroshimas

At the station exit, my bundle in hand,
Early the winter afternoon's wet snow
Falls thinly round me, out of a crudded sun.
I had forgotten to remember where I was.
Looking about, I see it might be anywhere –
A station, a town like any other in Japan,
Ramshackle, muddy, noisy, drab; a cheerfully
Shallow permanence: peeling concrete, litter, 'Atomic
Lotion, for hair fall-out,' a flimsy department-store;
Racks and towers of neon, flashy over tiled and tilted waves
Of little roofs, shacks cascading lemons and persimmons,
Oranges and dark-red apples, shanties awash with rainbows
Of squid and octopus, shellfish, slabs of tuna, oysters, ice,
Ablaze with fans of soiled nude-picture books
Thumbed abstractedly by schoolboys, with second-hand looks.

The river remains unchanged, sad, refusing rehabilitation.
In this long, wide, empty official boulevard
The new trees are still small, the office blocks
Basely functional, the bridge a slick abstraction.
But the river remains unchanged, sad, refusing rehabilitation.

In the city centre, far from the station's lively squalor,
A kind of life goes on, in cinemas and hi-fi coffee bars,
In the shuffling racket of pin-table palaces and parlours,
The souvenir-shops piled with junk, kimonoed kewpie-dolls,
Models of the bombed Industry Promotion Hall, memorial ruin
Tricked out with glitter-frost and artificial pearls.

Set in an awful emptiness, the modern tourist hotel is trimmed
With jaded Christmas frippery, flatulent balloons; in the hall,
A giant dingy iced cake in the shape of a Cinderella coach.
The contemporary stairs are treacherous, the corridors
Deserted, my room an overheated morgue, the bar in darkness.
Punctually, the electric chimes ring out across the tidy waste
Their doleful public hymn – the tune unrecognizable, evangelist.

Here atomic peace is geared to meet the tourist trade.
Let it remain like this, for all the world to see,
Without nobility or loveliness, and dogged with shame
That is beyond all hope of indignation. Anger, too, is dead.
And why should memorials of what was far
From pleasant have the grace that helps us to forget?

In the dying afternoon, I wander dying round the Park of Peace.
It is right, this squat, dead place, with its left-over air
Of an abandoned International Trade and Tourist Fair.
The stunted trees are wrapped in straw against the cold.
The gardeners are old, old women in blue bloomers, white
    aprons,
Survivors weeding the dead brown lawns around the Children's
    Monument.

A hideous pile, the Atomic Bomb Explosion Centre, freezing
    cold,
'Includes the Peace Tower, a museum containing
Atomic-melted slates and bricks, photos showing
What the Atomic Desert looked like, and other
Relics of the catastrophe.'

Continued ▶

The other relics:
The ones that made me weep;
The bits of burnt clothing,
The stopped watches, the torn shirts.
The twisted buttons,
The stained and tattered vests and drawers,
The ripped kimonos and charred boots,
The white blouse polka-dotted with atomic rain, indelible,
The cotton summer pants the blasted boys crawled home in,
    to bleed
And slowly die.

Remember only these.
They are the memorials we need.

James Kirkup

The Unexploded Bomb

Two householders (semi-detached) once found,
Digging their gardens, a bomb underground –
Half in one's land, half in t'other's, with the fence between.
Neighbours they were, but for years had been
Hardly on speaking terms. Now X unbends
To pass a remark across the creosoted fence:
'Look what I've got! . . . Oh, you've got it too.
Then what, may I ask, are you proposing to do
About this object of yours which menaces my wife,
My kiddies, my property, my whole way of life?'
'Your way of life,' says Y, 'is no credit to humanity.
I don't wish to quarrel; but since you began it, I
Find your wife stuck-up, your children repel me,
And let me remind you that we too have the telly.
This bomb of mine – '
                              'I don't like your tone!
And I must point out that, since I own
More bomb than you, to create any tension
Between us won't pay you.'
                              'What a strange misapprehension!'
Says the other: 'my portion of bomb is near
Six inches longer than yours. So there!'

'They seem,' the bomb muttered in its clenched and narrow
Sleep, 'to take me for a vegetable marrow.'
'It would give me,' said X, 'the very greatest pleasure
To come across the fence now with my tape-measure – '
'Oh no,' Y answered, 'I'm not having you
Trampling my flowerbeds and peering through
My windows.'

Continued ▶

'Oho,' snarled X, 'if that's
Your attitude, I warn you to keep your brats
In future from trespassing upon my land,
Or they'll bitterly regret it.'
                                'You misunderstand.
My family has no desire to step on
Your soil; and my bomb is a peace-lover's weapon.'

Called a passing angel, 'If you two shout
And fly into tantrums and keep dancing about,
The thing will go off. It is surely permissible
To say that your bomb, though highly fissible,
Is in another sense one and indivisible;
By which I mean – if you'll forgive the phrase,
Gentlemen – the bloody thing works both ways.
So let me put forward a dispassionate proposal:
Both of you, ring for a bomb-disposal
Unit, and ask them to remove post-haste
The cause of your dispute.'

                                X and Y stared aghast
At the angel. 'Remove my bomb?' they sang
In unison both: 'allow a gang
To invade my garden and pull up the fence
Upon which my whole way of life depends?
Only a sentimental idealist
Could moot it. I, thank God, am a realist.'
The angel fled. The bomb turned over
In its sleep and mumbled, 'I shall soon discover,
If X and Y are too daft to unfuse me,
How the Devil intends to use me.'

C. Day Lewis

Military Two-Step

(Expenditure on arms today has escalated to such a point that for each man, woman and child there is now 3.5 tons of TNT.)

You say your shack
needs restoration
the roof leaks
the walls crack
it's a rat & cock-
roach abomination.

Now don't you worry
you can always jive
with your 3.5
tons of TNT.

You say the children
are in dire need
of an education
they're bright & eager
but you can't afford
kindergarten or teacher.

Now don't you worry
you can always jive
with your 3.5
tons of TNT.

You say the family
is always hungry
there's no food
in the larder
& you have to walk
six scorching miles
for a pail of water.

Now don't you worry
you can always jive
with your 3.5
tons of TNT.

You say your daughter
died last month
from chronic cholera
she would've been saved
but you couldn't raise
the fees for a doctor.

Now don't you worry
you can always jive
with your 3.5
tons of TNT.

Cecil Rajendra

'A meteorite is reported to have landed in New England. No damage is said . . .'

A littlebit of heaven fell
From out the sky one day
It landed in the ocean
Not so very far away
The General at the radar screen
Rubbed his hands with glee
And grinning pressed the button
That started World War Three.

From every corner of the earth
Bombs began to fly
There were even missile jams
No traffic lights in the sky
In the time it takes to blow your nose
The people fell, the mushrooms rose

'House!' cried the fatlady
As the bingohall moved to various parts
of the town
'*Raus!*' cried the German butcher
as his shop came tumbling down

Philip was in the countinghouse
Counting out his money
The Queen was in the parlour
Eating bread and honey
When through the window
Flew a bomb
And made them go all funny

(By the way if you're wondering
What happened to the maid
Well in this particular raid
She lost more than her nose
In fact she came to a close
Or so the story goes.)

In the time it takes to draw a breath
Or eat a toadstool, instant death.

The rich
Huddled outside the doors of their fallout shelters
Like drunken carolsingers

The poor
Clutching shattered televisions
And last week's editions of TV Times
(but the very last)

Civil defence volunteers
With their tin hats in one hand
And their heads in the other

CND supporters
Their ban the bomb mojos beginning to rust
Have scrawled 'I told you so' in the dust

A littlebit of heaven fell
From the sky one day
It landed in Vermont
North-Eastern USA
The general at the radar screen
He should have got the sack
But that wouldn't bring
Three thousand million, seven hundred, and sixty-eight people back,
Would it?

Roger McGough

Inscribing the Circles

A smell of new paper
rises from the stripped pine table
where the map lies compact,
folded like a present waiting to be unwrapped.

Crisply, the paper rectangles
unfold like a Chinese box,
revealing a tessellation of oblongs
that acts almost as a tablecloth,
but not quite.

The pencil is attached to the compass,
practice passes are made in the air
above the map.
So it begins:
the inscribing of the circles.

Within a radius of three quarters of a mile
the prick of the compass spreads to a crater.

Within a radius of twenty miles
the buildings become as flat as the map.
Within a radius of forty miles
a pillar of fire magnetises a hurtle of winds.

Within a radius of one hundred miles
the bringing wind blows its slow seepage of death.

Within a radius of two hundred miles
stand those who, having looked, will never see again.

With the required degree of precision
ther compass moves silently again and again
until a neat pattern of concentric circles
marks the map like a target,
bisected by the lines
houses, schools, hospitals and factories
wait passively to be hit.

Frank Flynn

For sale: a portion of that building site
known as 'space'. A most desirable location.
Planning permission for –
laser beams, ray guns, particle dis-
integrators, missles air to earth.
Scope for *every* use.
Competition fierce – bid now!

(Only trouble is, it costs the Earth.)

Rosemary Southey

YOUR ATTENTION PLEASE –
The Polar DEW* has just warned that
A nuclear rocket strike of
At least one thousand megatons
Has been launched by the enemy
Directly at our major cities.
This announcement will take
Two and a quarter minutes to make,
You therefore have a further
Eight and a quarter minutes
To comply with the shelter
Requirements published in the Civil
Defence Code – section Atomic Attack.
A specially shortened Mass
Will be broadcast at the end
Of this announcement –
Protestant and Jewish services
Will begin simultaneously –
Select your wavelength immediately
According to instructions
In the Defence Code. Do not
Take well-loved pets (including birds)
Into your shelter – they will consume
Fresh air. Leave the old and bed-
Ridden, you can do nothing for them.
Remember to press the sealing
Switch when everyone is in
The shelter. Set the radiation
Aerial, turn on the geiger barometer.
Turn off your Television now.
Turn off your radio immediately
The services end. At the same time
Secure explosion plugs in the ears
Of each member of your family. Take
Down your plasma flasks. Give your children

The pills marked one and two
In the CD green container, then put
Them to bed. Do not break
The inside airlock seals until
The radiation All Clear shows
(Watch for the cuckoo in your
Perspex panel), or your District
Touring Doctor rings your bell.
If before this your air becomes
Exhausted or if any of your family
Is critically injured, administer
The capsules marked 'Valley Forge'
(Red pocket in No. 1 Survival Kit)
For painless death. (Catholics
Will have been instructed by their priests
What to do in this eventuality.)
This announcement is ending. Our President
Has already given orders for
Massive retaliation – it will be
Decisive. Some of us may die.
Remember, statistically
It is not likely to be you.
All flags are flying fully dressed
On Government buildings – the sun is shining.
Death is the least we have to fear.
We are all in the hands of God,
Whatever happens happens by His will.
Now go quickly to your shelters.

Peter Porter

*Distant Early Warning.

Refuse Cruise

Refuse Cruise
and Trident
they're so
unattractive
it's always
more fun
on a
beach
in the
sun
when the
breeze
is not
radio-
active.

Phil Vallack

In Favour of the Bomb

In a world that's full of hatred,
    and news that's always bad,
The dividing line gets thinner,
    who is sane and who is mad.
If a man thinks he's two people,
    is he the hopeless case?
Or the man who makes a bomb,
    which can destroy the Human Race?
The ones we deem are madmen,
    are in a padded cell,
But the madmen who are ruling,
    can turn our world to Hell!

Should we blindly follow leaders,
    like sheep, do as we're told?
And in war find our opposers,
    using weapons we have sold!
It's not worry of our weapons,
    Whether nuclear, big or small,
But the leaders of the countries,
    and the one who starts it all!

R. J. Latham

I sing
of the beauty of Athens
without its slaves

Of a world free
of kings and queens
and other remnants
of an arbitrary past

Of earth
with no
sharp north
or deep south
without blind curtains
or iron walls

Of the end
of warlords and armouries
and prisons of hate and fear

Of deserts treeing
and fruiting
after the quickening rains

Of the sun
radiating ignorance
and stars informing
nights of unknowing

I sing of a world reshaped

Niyi Osundare

Barely a twelvemonth after
The seven days war that put the world to sleep,
Late in the evening the strange horses came.
By then we had made our covenant with silence,
But in the first few days it was so still
We listened to our breathing and were afraid.
On the second day
The radios failed; we turned the knobs; no answer.
On the third day a warship passed us, heading north,
Dead bodies piled on the deck. On the sixth day
A plane plunged over us into the sea. Thereafter
Nothing. The radios dumb;
And still they stand in corners of our kitchens,
And stand, perhaps, turned on, in a million rooms
All over the world. But now if they should speak,
If on a sudden they should speak again,
If on the stroke of noon a voice should speak,
We would not listen, we would not let it bring
That bad old world that swallowed its children quick
At one great gulp. We would not have it again.
Sometimes we think of the nations lying asleep,
Curled blindly in impenetrable sorrow,
And then the thought confounds us with its strangeness.

The tractors lie about our fields; at evening
They look like dank sea-monsters crouched and waiting.
We leave them where they are and let them rust:
'They'll moulder away and be like other loam.'
We make our oxen drag our rusty ploughs,
Long laid aside. We have gone back
Far past our fathers' land.

                                    And then, that evening
Late in the summer the strange horses came.
We heard a distant tapping on the road,
A deepening drumming; it stopped, went on again,
And at the corner changed to hollow thunder.
We saw the heads
Like a wild wave charging and were afraid.
We had sold our horses in our fathers' time
To buy new tractors. Now they were strange to us
As fabulous steeds set on an ancient shield
Or illustrations in a book of knights.
We did not dare go near them. Yet they waited,
Stubborn and shy, as if they had been sent
By an old command to find our whereabouts
And that long-lost archaic companionship.
In the first moment we had never a thought
That they were creatures to be owned and used.
Among them were some half-a-dozen colts
Dropped in some wilderness of the broken world,
Yet new as if they had come from their own Eden.
Since then they have pulled our ploughs and borne our loads,
But that free servitude still can pierce our hearts.
Our life is changed; their coming our beginning.

Edwin Muir

THE VIETNAM WAR

American involvement in Vietnam began in the 1950s. By the mid sixties there were half a million Americans in Vietnam fighting the army of North Vietnam, sometimes called the Vietcong. Over a million Vietnamese were killed, in addition 1,400 villages and a quarter of the country's forests were destroyed. More bombs were dropped on North Vietnam than in the entire Second World War. As the costs of the war rose and world opinion turned against them, the Americans accepted peace terms in 1973. The war did not end until 1975.

Since the war, 60,000 Vietnam veterans have committed suicide, more than America lost in the war itself. Vietnam is still suffering the effects of 30 years of continuous war.

He was twelve years old,
and I do not know his name.
The mercenaries took him and his father,
whose name I do not know,
one morning upon the High plateau.
Green Beret looked down on the frail boy
with the eyes of a hurt animal and thought,
a good fright will make him talk.
He commanded, and the father was taken away
behind the forest's green wall.
'Right kid tell us where they are,
tell us where or your father – dead.'
With eyes now bright and filled with terror
the slight boy said nothing.
'You've got one minute kid', said Green Beret,
'tell us where or we kill father'
and thrust his wrist-watch against a face all eyes,
the second-hand turning, jerking on its way.
'OK boy ten seconds to tell us where they are'
In the last instant the silver hand shattered the
sky and the forest of trees.
'Kill the old guy' roared Green Beret
and shots hammered out
behind the forest's green wall
and sky and trees and soldiers stood
in silence, and the boy cried out.
Green Beret stood
in silence, as the boy crouched down
and shook with tears,
as children do when their father dies.

Continued ▶

Christ, said one mercenary to Green Beret,
'he didn't know a damn thing
we killed the old guy for nothing.'
So they all went away,
Green Beret and his mercenaries.

And the boy knew everything.
He knew everything about them, the caves,
the trails, the hidden places and the names,
and in the moment that he cried out,
in that same instant,
protected by frail tears
far stronger than any wall of steel,
they passed everywhere
like tigers
across the High Plateau.

Ho Thien

What Were They Like?

1) Did the people of Vietnam
    use lanterns of stone?
2) Did they hold ceremonies
    to reverence the opening of buds?
3) Were they inclined to quiet laughter?
4) Did they use bone and ivory,
    jade and silver, for ornament?
5) Had they an epic poem?
6) Did they distinguish between speech and singing?

1) Sir, their light hearts turned to stone.
    It is not remembered whether in gardens
    stone lanterns illumined pleasant ways.
2) Perhaps they gathered once to delight in blossom,
    but after the children were killed
    there were no more buds.
3) Sir, laughter is bitter to the burned mouth.
4) A dream ago, perhaps. Ornament is for joy.
    All the bones were charred.
5) It is not remembered. Remember,
    most were peasants; their life
    was in rice and bamboo.
    When peaceful clouds were reflected in the paddies
    and the water buffalo stepped surely along terraces,
    maybe fathers told their sons old tales.
    When bombs smashed those mirrors
    there was time only to scream.
6) There is an echo yet
    of their speech which was like a song.
    It was reported their singing resembled
    the flight of moths in moonlight.
    Who can say? It is silent now.

Denise Levertov

Written at the start of one of our bombing pauses over North Vietnam.

How come nobody is being bombed today?
I want to know, being a citizen
of this country and a family man.
You can't take my fate in your hands,
without informing me.
I can blow up a bomb or crush a skull –
whoever started this peace
without advising me
through a news leak
at which I could have voiced a protest,
running my whole family off a cliff.

David Ignatow

To Whom It May Concern

I was run over by the truth one day.
Ever since the accident I've walked this way
　　So stick my legs in plaster
　　Tell me lies about Vietnam.

Heard the alarm clock screaming with pain,
Couldn't find myself so I went back to sleep again
　　So fill my ears with silver
　　Stick my legs in plaster
　　Tell me lies about Vietnam.

Every time I shut my eyes all I see is flames.
Made a marble phone book and I carved all the names
　　So coat my eyes with butter
　　Fill my ears with silver
　　Stick my legs in plaster
　　Tell me lies about Vietnam.

I smell something burning, hope it's just my brains.
They're only dropping peppermints and daisy-chains
　　So stuff my nose with garlic
　　Coat my eyes with butter
　　Fill my ears with silver
　　Stick my legs in plaster
　　Tell me lies about Vietnam.

Where were you at the time of the crime?
Down by the Cenotaph drinking slime
　　So chain my tongue with whisky
　　Stuff my nose with garlic
　　Coat my eyes with butter
　　Fill my ears with silver
　　Stick my legs in plaster
　　Tell me lies about Vietnam.

You put your bombers in, you put your conscience out,
You take the human being and you twist it all about
    So scrub my skin with women
    Chain my tongue with whisky
    Stuff my nose with garlic
    Coat my eyes with butter
    Fill my ears with silver
    Stick my legs in plaster
    Tell me lies about Vietnam.

Adrian Mitchell

These days,
like you, I am an expert in disbelief.
War in Vietnam and Peace in America
have imbued in us a God-like detachment;
a perceptual handicap,
which interdicts most lies.
For us,
neither the president,
nor the emperor,
wears clothes.

It begins with simply this:
that each man goes to his war
as he goes to his love; alone.
And from neither does he return as before.
For love and war exist
at the edges of the human experience
and whether new-born or quick-dead,
life hangs in the balance.
Either way, man grapples with his universe
at the very limits of social restraint.
His cultural upbringing.
too weak to govern
in the province of the darkness
and the dawn.

To survive in combat
a man must turn
from the teachings of other men
and come face to face with himself.

For some it is a joy
to come to know such a man as he is.
For others, it is a nightmare
which recurs so long as he may live.

Steve Mason

THE FALKLANDS WAR

The Falkland Islands are in the South Atlantic near to the coast of Argentina. The Argentinians have long claimed the islands as theirs and invaded on 2 April 1982. The Falklands have been ruled by Britain for 200 years and a Task Force set sail to recapture the islands. This was achieved on 14 June 1982. Ships, planes and troops were lost on both sides. Britain had 255 men killed and 777 wounded. Argentina lost about 1000 men. The financial cost of the war to Britain is estimated at £2 billion.

Dawn Attack

Steam rises off of their bodies,
Their faces are tired and drawn.
Their feet still hurt from the marching they've done,
And their clothes are muddy and torn.
They drink their tea or have a last smoke,
As they wait for the first light of dawn.

'On your feet lads', whispers the Sergeant,
'Come on we're out on the right!'
They quietly pick up their weapons,
The ones they've been cleaning all night.
Then silently follow him into the mist,
Until the last man's out of sight.

The whistle and crump of mortars is heard,
The Artillery thunders away.
An explosion close by, but we're safe in the trench,
It was probably only a stray.
The radio's dead, what's wrong on the right?
We stand there and silently pray.

Then suddenly all becomes quiet,
'The mist's clearing', our Captain said.
'Come on lads, it's time to move forward'.
In my stomach a feeling of dread,
Then we move out, on the right, to the valley,
To pick up our wounded and dead.

Continued ▶

Continued ▶

Steam rises off of their bodies,
Their faces no longer look drawn.
There's no pain in their feet from the marching they did,
Though their clothes are still muddy and torn.
Now they've drunk their last drink and had their last smoke,
And they'll never again see a dawn.

R. J. Latham

9th Parachute Squadron, Royal Engineers.

There were no heroes here
Amongst the men who tramped through
Rutted, quaking moor,
Or crawled, cat-silent,
Over skittering scree
To prove the way.

No heroes fought the blazing fires
Which sucked the very blood from
Ship and man alike.
Or braved knife cold
Without a thought
To save a life.

No heroes they, but ones who loved
Sweet life and children's laugh,
And dreamt of home
When war allowed.
They were but men.

David Morgan

Sea Harrier pilot, Royal Navy.

My Family

Did you see us on the telly, Mum?
When we sailed away –
Laughing, waving, cheering
Like in films of yesterday.

Did you read it in *The Sun*, Pop?
How we pasted them first time.
You told me all about your war.
What do you think of mine?

Did you get the letters home, dear?
How I missed you and was sad.
Did you give my love to Tracy?
Does she miss her funny Dad?

Did you see us on the hillside?
Could you spot which one was me?
Were the flowers very heavy
For a grown up girl of three?

Paul D. Wapshott

formerly Parachute Regiment.

THE Sun

uesday, May 4, 1982   14p   TODAY'S TV: PAGE 12

QE2 IS SET TO SAIL FOR WAR

Liner may be turned back from a cruise

We told you first

NINE days ago The Sun said that the QE3 was to be called up. Everybody denied it. Yesterday the Ministry of Defence confirmed it. If you really want to know what's going on in the war buy The Sun. We try harder. See Page 2.

GOTCHA

SUNK — AN Argie patrol boat like this one was sunk by missiles from Royal Navy helicopters after first opening fire on our lads

Our lads sink gunboat and hole cruiser

From TONY SNOW aboard HMS Invincible

THE NAVY had the Argies on their knees last night after a devastating double punch.

WALLOP: They torpedoed the 14,000-ton Argentina cruiser General-Belgrano and left it a useless wreck.

BATTLE FOR THE

The Sun headlines were *Gotcha*
and seventeen year olds
acted out a bare-bones play.

They envied those there –
the regulars who'd signed up
into the real thing.

It would all be finished
before they had a run
at the Argies, alas.

They buried the *Belgrano*,
sank it over and over
in a London classroom –

cheering, holding up their papers
to calls of *Gotcha*,
and walked on waves, no surrender.

Katherine Gallagher

Tea-time in Portsmouth 1982

The news comes pouring as she runs from school.
'We made some cakes. There's fifteen pence to pay.
We had an awful dinner. It was yuk!
I got a star in history today.

You know that girl with glasses and long hair,
Who said this year they're going to Italy?
They won't be going now. She's been away.
Her Dad was on the *Sheffield*. What's for tea?'

Margaret Hothi

Today, I am a tourist in my own town;
these crowded streets look dark and strange,
a new cold wind tugs flags and bright leaves,
my cheeks are tight with tears,
and familiar faces round me
are changed by pride or grief.

As the regiments go by
our hearts all beat in time
with drums
and the silent feet of marching men.

And we can have no more to say
about the rights and wrongs of war
than this little trotting mascot pony:
like him, our heads are held by gold-braid men,
and our feet cannot resist the music.

Jean Hathaway

We Shall Remember Them

*(Written in September 1984 following an account on
BBC Radio 4 by the mother of a boy killed in the
Falklands War.)*

No visit to a gracious Queen,
no presentation honouring the dead.

The day his medal came
her fingers fumbled with the padded envelope;
ribbon and steel dropped from her hand,
another piece rolled out of sight.

When they came home they found her there,
tears falling on the polished floor,
trying to fit the fragments of her son,
to make sense of the scattered jigsaw
of his life.

Home-assembly decoration kits
by order of a grateful Government,
broken like the bodies
they were made to celebrate.

But then he was, at seventeen, hardly a soldier.
Just a name and number in the power game.
Mail-order hero of a battle scene.

Sheila Parry

(Written after watching the Robert Lawrence/Richard Eyre film on BBC TV, June 1988, remembering preceding and succeeding comment.)

Why should he laugh? A boy
Grown old upon the mountainside.
Who shall tell him of triumph?
Why should his fire, raging
At the mountain top, abate?

If he has sparked
A question to the heart
Of those that deal in war,
His loss might be worth living for,
And reappraisal not too late.

Margaret J. Tiddy

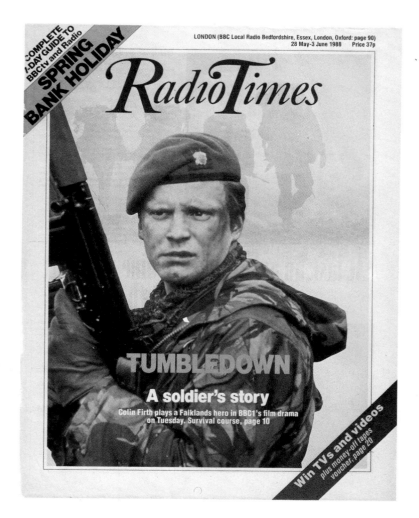

LONDON (BBC Local Radio Bedfordshire, Essex, London, Oxford: page 90)
28 May-3 June 1988   Price 37p

Radio Times

TUMBLEDOWN

A soldier's story

Colin Firth plays a Falklands hero in BBC1's film drama
on Tuesday. Survival course, page 10

IRELAND

Conflict in Ireland has a long history but the current 'troubles' started in the late 1960s. The British army was sent to protect the Catholic from the Protestant community. Since then sectarian conflict between the two communities has escalated. The war between the Irish Republican Army and the British Army has continued alongside the horrors of internment, hunger strikes, bombings and civilian deaths.

Loyalists seek to retain the link with Britain, whereas Republicans want a united Ireland. Neither side sees room for compromise. Some 2,500 people have been killed to date.

He would drink by himself
And raise a weathered thumb
Towards the high shelf,
Calling another rum
And blackcurrant, without
Having to raise his voice,
Or order a quick stout
By a lifting of the eyes
And a discreet dumb-show
Of pulling off the top;
At closing time would go
In waders and peaked cap
Into the showery dark,
A dole-kept breadwinner
But a natural for work.
I loved his whole manner,
Sure-footed but too sly,
His deadpan sidling tact,
His fisherman's quick eye
And turned observant back.

Incomprehensible
To him, my other life.
Sometimes, on his high stool,
Too busy with his knife
At a tobacco plug
And not meeting my eye,
In the pause after a slug
He mentioned poetry.
We would be on our own
And, always politic
And shy of condescension,
I would manage by some trick
To switch the talk to eels
Or lore of the horse and cart
Or the Provisionals.

But my tentative art
His turned back watches too:
He was blown to bits
Out drinking in a curfew
Others obeyed, three nights
After they shot dead
The thirteen men in Derry.
PARAS THIRTEEN, the walls said,
BOGSIDE NIL. That Wednesday
Everybody held
His breath and trembled.

Seamus Heaney

At alarming bell daybreak, before
Scraping of cats or windows creaking over the street,
Eleven miles of road between them,
The enemy commanders synchronised their heartbeats:
Seven forty-five by the sun.
At ten the soldiers were climbing into lorries,
Asthmatic engines drawing breath in even shifts.
The others were fretting over guns
Counting up ammunition and money.
At eleven they lay in wait at the cross
With over an hour to go.
The pine trees looked up stiff;
At the angle of the road, polished stones
Forming a stile, a knowing path
Twisting away: the rough grass
Gripped the fragments of the wall.
A small deep stream glassily descended:
Ten minutes to the hour.
The clouds grew grey, the road grey as iron,
The hills dark, the trees deep,
The fields faded; like white mushrooms
Sheep remote under the wind.
The stream ticked and throbbed
Nearer; a boy carried a can to the well
Nearer on the dark road.
The driver saw the child's back,
Nearer; the birds shoaled off the branches in fright.

Deafly rusting in the stream
The lorry now is soft as a last night's dream.
The soldiers and the deaf child
Landed gently in the water
They were light between long weeds
Settled and lay quiet, nobody
To listen to them now.
They all looked the same face down there:
Water too thick and deep to see.

They were separated for good.
It was cold, their teeth shrilling.
They slept like falling hay in waves.
Shells candied their skin; the water
Lay heavy and they could not rise but coiled
By scythefuls limply in ranks.
A long winter stacks their bodies
And words above their stillness hang from hooks
In skeins, like dark nets drying,
Flapping against the stream.
A watch vibrates alone in the filtering light;
Flitters of hair wave at the sun.

Eiléan Ni Chuilleanáin

One morning early I met armoured cars
In convoy, warbling along on powerful tyres,
All camouflaged with broken alder branches,
And headphoned soldiers standing up in turrets.
How long were they approaching down my roads
As if they owned them? The whole country was sleeping.
I had rights-of-way, fields, cattle in my keeping,
Tractors hitched to buckrakes in open sheds,
Silos, chill gates, wet slates, the greens and reds
Of outhouse roofs. Whom should I run to tell
Among all of those with their back doors on the latch
For the bringer of bad news, that small-hours visitant
Who, by being expected, might be kept distant?
Sowers of seed, erectors of headstones . . .
O charioteers, above your dormant guns,
It stands here still, stands vibrant as you pass,
The invisible, untoppled omphalos.*

Seamus Heaney

*omphalos: noun
  Literal meaning: decoration on a shield, or a sacred stone of
                            conical shape.
  Figurative meaning: centre or core.

So you think it's Stephen?
Then I'd best make sure
Be on the safe side as it were.
Ah, there's been a mistake. The hair
you see, it's black, now Stephen's fair . . .
What's that? The explosion?
Of course, burnt black. Silly of me.
I should have known. Then let's get on.

The face, is that a face I ask?
That mask of charred wood
blistered, scarred could
that have been a child's face?
The sweater, where intact, looks
in fact all too familiar.
But one must be sure.

The scoutbelt. Yes that's his.
I recognize the studs he hammered in
not a week ago. At the age
when boys get clothes-conscious
now you know. Its almost
certainly Stephen. But one must
be sure. Remove all trace of doubt.
Pull out every splinter of hope.

Pockets. Empty the pockets.
Handkerchief? Could be any schoolboy's.
Dirty enough. Cigarettes?
Oh this can't be Stephen.
I don't allow him to smoke you see.
He wouldn't disobey me. Not his father.

But that's his penknife. That's his alright.
And that's his key on the keyring
Gran gave him just the other night.
So this must be him.

I think I know what happened
.   .   .   .   .   .   about the cigarettes
No doubt he was minding them
for one of the older boys.
Yes that's it.
That's him.
That's our Stephen.

Roger McGough

Here are two pictures from my father's head –
I have kept them like secrets until now:
First, the Ulster Division at the Somme
Going over the top with
'No Surrender!': a boy about to die,
Screaming 'Give 'em one for the Shankill!'
'Wilder than Gurkhas' were my father's words
Of admiration and bewilderment.
Next comes the London-Scottish padre
Resettling kilts with his swagger-stick,
With a stylish backhand and a prayer.
Over a landscape of dead buttocks
My father followed him for fifty years.
At last, a belated casualty,
He said – lead traces flaring till they hurt –
'I am dying for King and Country, slowly.'
I touched his hand, his thin head I touched.

Now, with military honours of a kind,
With his badges, his medals like rainbows,
His spinning compass, I bury beside him
Three teenage soldiers, bellies full of
Bullets and Irish beer, their flies undone.
A packet of Woodbines I throw in,
A lucifer, the Sacred heart of Jesus
Paralysed as heavy guns put out
The night-light in a nursery for ever;

Also a bus-conductor's uniform –
He collapsed beside his carpet-slippers
Without a murmur, shot through the head
By a shivering boy who wandered in
Before they could turn the television down
Or tidy away the supper dishes.
To the children, to a bewildered wife,
I think 'Sorry Missus' was what he said.

Michael Longley

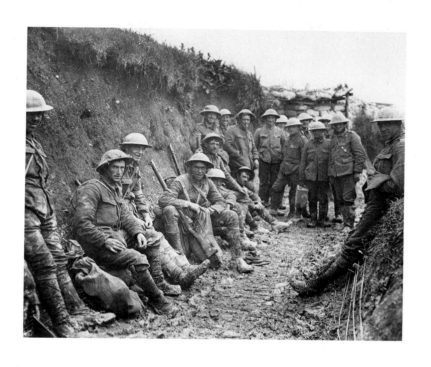

Reading and Responding to the Poems

1 A First Read

A poem needs to be read two or three times to get a sense of its meaning and, preferably, it should be read aloud. Reading aloud helps you get a feel of the rhythm and mood of a poem and to develop your own response. If you can work with someone, or in a group, then you can read the poem to each other and compare your versions.

- Did you read the poem at the same pace, or in the same tone of voice?
- Did you have the same sense of who was writing the poem and for whom it was intended?
- Did you agree on the theme of the poem?
- Did you find you were sympathetic to the poem's theme?
- Did you like it?

Listen to the reading on the audio cassette:

- What do you think of that?
- How does it compare with your reading?

ASSIGNMENT

In a pair, or group, choose three or four poems to read aloud to each other. You could choose:

- Poems by the same author (e.g. Wilfrid Owen, Vernon Scannell).
- Poems of a particular war (e.g. The Falklands).
- Poems about part of a war (e.g. trench warfare).
- Poems that all have a slightly humourous tone (e.g. 'Munition Wages', 'Lament of a Desert Rat', 'Icarus Allsorts').

Read, compare, discuss the poems and make notes on the discussion. Your notes should include:

- The content of each poem.
- The aspect of war each poem is concerned with.
- Similarities and differences in tone and style.
- Who is speaking the poem? Is it the author, or another voice?
- What it is about them that would interest a reader.
- What difficulties a reader might have understanding them.

Assemble your poems as if they were in an anthology and use your notes to write an introduction. Select some photographs or pictures to put with the poems and you will have constructed your own poetry anthology.

2 Closer Reading

There are a number of strategies that can help you get to grips with a poem. Once again, it helps a lot if you work with someone else.

a TITLES AND FIRST LINES

Sometimes it is worth spending a few minutes jotting down ideas that you get from reading the title or the first line of a poem. What for example do you think of with the title 'The Send-Off', or with the first line 'The Sun Headline said Gotcha'?

b WORDS OMITTED

Ask your partner to read a poem in which you have deleted a number of key words. Explain what words have been deleted but not their original place in the poem. Ask your partner to select a word for each gap. When your partner has done this, discuss the clues that determined the choice.

Here's a very brief example:

O! ancient   curse
Corrode, consume
Give back this universe
Its   bloom.

Pristine Crimson

The meaning is the most important factor, but an understanding of alliteration will also help.

c SEQUENCING

Offer a poem to your partner with the lines in the wrong order. Ask your partner to rewrite the poem in an order that makes the best sense. Then compare with the original version. Try it with the poem 'Breakfast', or 'All Quiet'.

You can also experiment with all the verses in the wrong sequence. Try it with 'Elegy for an 88 Gunner' or 'I Sing of Change'. Ask your partner to unravel the poem.

Note: these activities may just seem like games, but they force you to think carefully about the meaning of a poem as you reconstruct it. When you have completed one of these activities, you are in a stronger position to say: 'Now I understand what the poem is about.'

d QUESTIONING A POEM

Make a copy of a poem on a piece of paper and then jot down your comments and questions beside it (see 'The Send-Off') as you read. When you have finished, make a list of questions about the poem that you would set for another student to answer.

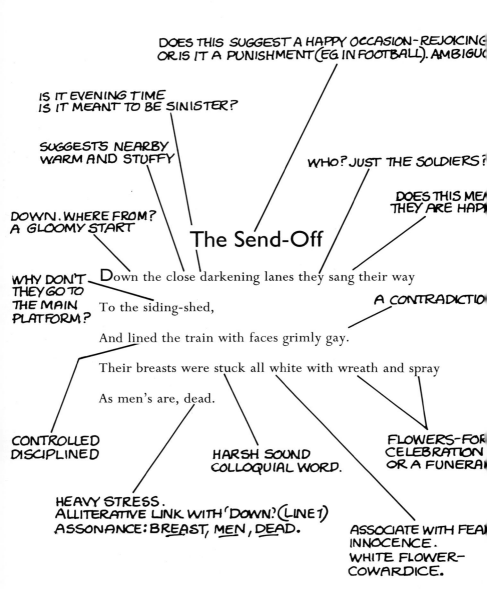

DOES THIS SUGGEST A HAPPY OCCASION - REJOICING
OR IS IT A PUNISHMENT (EG IN FOOTBALL). AMBIGUO

IS IT EVENING TIME
IS IT MEANT TO BE SINISTER?

SUGGESTS NEARBY
WARM AND STUFFY

WHO? JUST THE SOLDIERS?

DOES THIS MEA
THEY ARE HAP!

DOWN. WHERE FROM?
A GLOOMY START

The Send-Off

WHY DON'T
THEY GO TO
THE MAIN
PLATFORM?

Down the close darkening lanes they sang their way

To the siding-shed,

A CONTRADICTIO

And lined the train with faces grimly gay.

Their breasts were stuck all white with wreath and spray

As men's are, dead.

CONTROLLED
DISCIPLINED

HARSH SOUND
COLLOQUIAL WORD.

FLOWERS-FOR
CELEBRATION
OR A FUNERA!

HEAVY STRESS.
ALLITERATIVE LINK WITH 'DOWN? (LINE 1)
ASSONANCE: BREAST, MEN, DEAD.

ASSOCIATE WITH FEA!
INNOCENCE.
WHITE FLOWER-
COWARDICE.

Notes: There is a lot of information in these few lines about
soldiers catching a train and setting off for the front-line.
The rhythm and the rhyme make it seem tightly knit. Much
use of alliteration and assonance to hold it all together.
Sombre, gloomy mood.

ASSIGNMENT

Continue your own questioning of 'The Send-Off' with the full text. Consider what questions to set at the end and write out five of them.

Use these notes and your questions as the first draft for a review of the poem. Then redraft.

Alternatively, do the same with a poem of your choice.

3 Further Assignments

a 1914–1918 THE FIRST WORLD WAR

■ Use as many poems as you like for reference and write about the wartime experiences of (i) a young soldier who goes to the Front, and (ii) a young girl who goes to work in a munitions factory. Make use of the photographs, if you wish.

■ Rose Macaulay's poem 'Many Sisters to Many Brothers' is in the form of a letter to her brother. Use the poems written at the Front to help you reply, either in the form of a letter, or a poem.

■ Read either 'The Deserter' or 'Munition Wages'. Use either poem as the basis for a story about the particular characters portrayed.

■ Use the style, tone or structure of any of these poems as a model for your own poem. You could, for example, begin: 'Whenever war is spoken of, I find . . .'

b 1939–1945 THE SECOND WORLD WAR

■ Use the first four poems and the last poem in this section to write: 'A child's experience of World War Two'. You could discuss with relatives perhaps and make use of other stories, plays, or of television programmes you have watched.

■ With reference to the four poems about desert warfare, either: write a newspaper report describing the conditions there to people in Britain; or: compare the conditions and the poetry with those from the trenches in World War One.

■ In 'The Great War', Vernon Scannell recalled the images and events of World War Two. Using the poems of World War Two, write down those things that most strike you about this war. You could write in the form of a poem, or a piece of prose. Think about what happened to people as well as to places.

c 1945–1989 HIROSHIMA AND THE NUCLEAR AGE

■ With reference to three or four poems write about the likely effects, physical, mental and emotional, of a nuclear bomb exploding. You can also make use of the photographs.

■ 'Your Attention Please' is intended to read like the final radio message before a nuclear attack. Use the poem as a model for writing your own version.

■ Rewrite the events described in 'The Horses' as prose narrative and continue the story in any way you wish.

■ Say what you think. Express your views on nuclear weapons in the form of a story, an essay, a poem, or a play for radio. You could refer to stories you have read as well as the poems in this book.

d WAR IN OUR TIME: VIETNAM, THE FALKLANDS, IRELAND

■ Use either 'Green Beret', 'Dawn Attack', or 'Site of Ambush' as the basis for a story. Make use of the photographs for descriptions.

■ The way the media covers war is obviously important and sometimes controversial. Choose any two poems and use each as the basis for two conflicting newspaper reports.

■ Use any one of the poems as a model for writing your own. You could adopt the structure of 'What Were They Like?', or the situation in 'We Shall Remember Them', for example.

Alternatively, express your responses to one or more of the poems in the form of a statement: What I like about the following poem(s). You may want to do some close and careful reading before you start, perhaps with a partner.

e THE LANGUAGE OF WAR

■ Discuss and write about how far the language of war poetry has changed, or not, since 1914. You will want to consider:

the change in vocabulary or diction. Use the chart on page 126 as well,
the change in structure and length of poems,
the use of rhyme and of rhyming couplets,
the rhythm and mood of the poems,
the tone of the writers,
the difference between men and women poets,
why some concerns have changed and others have not.

Some Useful Terms for Discussing Poetry

Alliteration	The repetition of the initial consonant. E.g. '. . . crimson curse' ('On Receiving News of the War').
Ambiguity	The possibility of more than one meaning. E.g. 'The Send-Off'.
Assonance	The repetition of a vowel sound. E.g. '. . . untoppled omphalos' ('The Toome Road').
Couplets	Pairs of lines linked by rhyme. E.g. 'Suicide in the Trenches'.
Diction	The choice of words for a poem. E.g.

	Classical diction:	'Now God be thanked Who has matched us with His hour' ('Peace').
	Conversational diction:	'I've learned to wash in petrol tins and shave myself in tea' ('Lament of a Desert Rat').
	Poetic diction:	'No sound same swishing sea is heard' ('Convoy Episode').

Form	i) The type of poem. E.g. narrative, descriptive. 'Your Attention Please' is written in the form of a radio accouncement.
	ii) The structure of the poem. E.g. a fourteen-line sonnet ('Peace'), or continuous free verse ('Green Beret').

Imagery	The use of words to create pictures or images. E.g. '. . . Marilyn's skirts' ('August 6, 1945').
Irony	Words have the opposite meaning to what is written, as indicated by the tone. E.g. the poem 'Small Ad'.
Metaphor	The linking of two unlikely things. E.g. 'wove stories with tinsel thread' ('Evacuee').
Mood	The atmosphere of a poem. E.g. sombre, tragic, comic, joyful, romantic. This is different to the *tone* of a poem, which refers to the poet's attitude. E.g. bitter, angry, resentful, cynical, sad, ironic, mocking.
Pun	A comic effect suggesting two meanings from one word or phrase. E.g. 'Icarus Allsorts'.
Rhythm	The pace at which it seems appropriate to read a poem. Many poets vary the rhythm of a poem to *stress* certain words and thereby make the meaning more clear.
Satire	The use of wit or humour to attack something. E.g. the poem 'Refuse Cruise'.
Simile	A metaphor in which the relationship is expressed using 'like' or 'as'. E.g. 'We saw the herds/Like a wild wave charging' ('The Horses').

Note: Only use these terms if you are confident about their meaning. They are useful, but not essential, for discussing poetry.

The Semantic Field of War

Anglo-Saxon Bow, arrow, sword, shield, spear, fight, weapon

Middle English castle, army, navy, battle, war, peace, enemy, fighter, ambush, armour, artillery, cross-bow, lance, pike, pole-axe, hauberk, buckler, mace, gun, admiral, skirmish, archer, soldier, spy, chivalry (cavalry)

c. 1500–1549 trench, longbow, ordnance, redcoat, cannon, armada, harquebus, salvo, hussar

c. 1550–1599 mortar, bomb, bombadier, pistol, petard, infantry, fireship, calibre, volley

c. 1600–1649 grenade, musket, missile, rocket, carbine

c. 1650–1699 bayonet, blunderbus, shell, recruit, grenadier

c. 1700–1749 armament, howitzer, salute (artillery), blockade, press gang

c. 1750–1799 uniform, civilian, manoeuvre, grapeshot, rifle, martinet

c. 1800–1849 guerrilla, torpedo, shrapnel, diehard

c. 1850–1899 balaclava, cardigan, raglan, jingoism, Gatling gun, machine gun, mine (naval), magenta, solferino, war widow, Maxim gun, mauser, Red Cross, Tommy (Atkins), battleship, submarine, hand grenade

c. 1900–1949 concentration camp, khaki, mafick, submarine, destroyer, sam browne, tank, air-raid, bomber, fighter, strafe, depth charge, anti-aircraft, aircraft carrier, D-day, atomic bomb, camouflage, zeppelin, U-boat, flame-thrower, poison gas, rocketry, Hitler, scorched earth, total war, blitz, flak, ack-ack, prang, fire bomb, doodlebug, guided missile, ground/air to air missile, bren, sten, snafu, napalm, nuclear bomb, warhead, ground zero, paratroop, G.I. Joe, holocaust, Quisling, Resistance

c. 1950–1989 Cold War, Iron Curtain, bazooka, silo, defoliation, air-support, pacification, Exocet, heat-seeking missile, neutron bomb, chemical warfare

Index of Authors

Bedford, Madeline Ida 24
Brooke, Rupert 10
Chuilleanáin, Eiléan Ni 108
Douglas, Keith 44
Fell, Alison 59
Flynn, Frank 70
Gibson, Wilfrid 15
Hathaway, Jean 100
Heaney, Seamus 106, 110
Henderson, Hamish 46
Henri, Adrian 33
Herbert, Zbigniew 52
Hodgson, W. N. 11
Hothi, Margaret 99
Houston, Libby 55
Gallagher, Katherine 98
Ignatow, David 85
Jennings, Elizabeth 32
Kirkup, James 62
Latham, R. J. 75, 93
Ledward, Patricia 49
Letts, Winifred 22
Levertov, Denise 84
Lewis, C. Day 65
Longley, Michael 114
Lowbury, Edward 60
Macaulay, Rose 25
Mackintosh, E. A. 13

Mason, Steve 88
Mayo, Frances 50
McGough, Roger 112
Meddemmen, J. G. 40
Milne, A. A. 27
Mitchell, Adrian 86
Morgan, David 95
Muir, Edwin 78
Osundare, Niyi 77
Owen, Wilfrid 14, 16, 20
Parry, Sheila 101
Pope, Jessie 23
Porter, Peter 72
Rajendra, Cecil 67
Reed, Henry 39
Robinson, Charles 48
Rosenberg, Isaac 12, 18
Różewicz, Tadeusz 51
Sassoon, Siegfried 19, 21, 26
Scannell, Vernon 28, 38, 54
Southey, Rosemary 71
Thien, Ho 82
Thrilling, Isobel 34, 36
Tiddy, Margaret J. 102
Trapnell, N. J. 42
Vallack, Phil 74
Wapshott, Paul D. 96
Wedge, John 47

Acknowledgements

Recordings on an accompanying cassette (ISBN 0 582 05812 0; only available to schools) are taken from the BBC School Radio series GCSE English: The Poetry of War. The series was co-produced by Simon Fuller and Colin Smith.

The front cover is adapted from a poster designed to promote a national poetry competition in 1989. The competition was organised by BBC School Radio and the Imperial War Museum. Original design by Pentagram.

Acknowledgement is due to the following, whose permission is due for multiple reproduction:
page 15 Macmillan, London and Basingstoke, from 'Collected poems, 1905–25'; **19** Mr G. Sassoon; **21** Mr G. Sassoon; **25** A. D. Peters & Co Ltd, from 'In time of war' published by Blackie; **26** Mr G. Sassoon; **28** Vernon Scannell, from 'In time of war' published by Blackie; **32** David Higham Associates; **33** Rogers, Coleridge and White Ltd, from 'In time of war' published by Blackie; **34** Isobel Thrilling; **36** Isobel Thrilling; **38** Vernon Scannell, from 'Soldiering on' published by Robson Books Ltd; **39** Henry Reed; **40** J. G. Meddemmen; **42** The Salamander Oasis Trust; **44** Keith Douglas; **46** Hamish Henderson, from 'Poems of the Second World War. The oasis selection'; **47** J. M. Dent & Sons Ltd, from 'Poems of the Second World War'; **48** The Salamander Oasis Trust; **49** Patricia Ledward, from 'Poems of the Second World War. The oasis selection'; **51** Rapp & Whiting Limited; **54** Vernon Scannell, from 'Soldiering on' published by Robson Books Ltd; **55** Libby Houston; **59** Peake Associates, from 'Poems for peace' edited by Linda Hoy, published by Pluto; **60** Edward Lowbury; **62** James Kirkup, from 'Touchstone 5' edited by M. G. and P. Benton published by Hodder & Stoughton; **65** A. D. Peters & Co Ltd, from 'Conflicts 2' published by Nelson; **68** A. D. Peters & Co Ltd, from 'Modern Poets Ten' published by Penguin; **70** Frank Flynn; **71** Rosemary Southey, from 'Poems for peace' edited by Linda Hoy published by Pluto; **72** Peter Porter; **74** Pluto Publishing Ltd, from 'Poems for peace' edited by Linda Hoy published by Pluto; **75** R. J. Latham; **77** Niyi Osundare, from 'Modern African poetry' edited by Moore & Beier; **78** Faber & Faber Ltd, from 'The collected poems of Edwin Muir'; **84** Laurence Pollinger Ltd; **95** David Morgan; **96** Paul D. Wapshott; **98** Katherine Gallagher; **99** Margaret Hothi; **100** Jean Hathaway; **101** Sheila Parry; **102** Margaret J. Tiddy; **106** Faber & Faber Ltd, from 'Fieldwork' published by Faber; **108** Bloodaxe Books, from 'The second voyage'; **110** Faber & Faber Ltd, from 'Fieldwork' published by Faber; **112** A. D. Peters & Co Ltd, from 'Gig' published by Jonathan Cape; **114** Michael Longley.
The Publishers have made every attempt to trace the copyright holders, but in cases where they may have failed will be pleased to make the necessary arrangements at the first opportunity.

We are also grateful to the following for permission to reproduce photographs:
page 8 Imperial War Museum; **15** Mary Evans Picture Library; **17** Imperial War Museum; **21** Imperial War Museum/Robert Hunt Library; **23, 35** and **37** Imperial War Museum; **43** and **45** Imperial War Museum/Robert Hunt Library; **48** Hulton Picture Company; **58** and **61** Imperial War Museum; **68, 69** and **71** United States Information Service; **74** BBC copyright; **76** John Sanford/Science Photo Library; **81** Associated Press; **83** and **89** United Press International; **92** and **94** Imperial War Museum; **99** Press Association; **103** BBC/Radio Times; **104** Hulton Picture Company; **107** Chris Steele Perkins/Magnum; **111** Hulton Picture Company; **115** Imperial War Museum.

First published 1990

© The author and BBC Enterprises Limited/Longman Group UK Limited 1989

Book design by **Keith Crawford**

Published by BBC Books and Longman Group UK Limited
BBC Books, a division of BBC Enterprises Limited
Woodlands
80 Wood Lane
London W12 0TT

Longman Group UK Limited
Longman House
Burnt Mill
Harlow
Essex CM20 2JE
England and Associated Companies throughout the World

ISBN 0 582 05811 2

Set in Perpetua
Typeset by Ace Filmsetting Ltd, Frome
Text printed in Britain by Bell & Bain
Cover origination by Richard Clay Ltd
Cover printed by Fletchers